ADDICTION-HACKS

There's Simply No Way to Fail

William Nixon

ADDICTION-HACKS©

There's simply, No Way to Fail©

STANDARD EDITION

©2019 WILLIAM NIXON

Paperback ISBN 978-1-7336343-0-4

eBook ISBN 978-1-7336343-1-1

DISCLAIMER

As Required by Law, (because politicians and lawyers say they're looking out for us) please note, that while we are sharing information, products, services etc. through this website, email, newsletters, podcasts, Twitter accounts, Facebook pages and other medium, the below statement should be read and understood.

I will make every effort to ensure the accuracy of the products and services on this or any other site that I have influence or control over. It is impossible to guarantee results as I am not you. I cannot guarantee your future results and or success and cannot foresee your future. I will do everything in my power to help you reach your potential and your goals.

All media content provided on this site, in our books or on audio downloads/CDs, etc. is intended for entertainment purposes only. We are not affiliated with any health agencies. None of our content is intended to offer medical or health related advice and must never be used as such. Our content is not a substitute for a qualified medical consultation or medical advice of any type. Never make alterations to any medicines or health regimens that you may be on without first consulting your doctor or qualified medical professional. We accept no responsibility or liability whatsoever for any injury, loss or damage in any shape or form incurred in part or in whole as a direct result of any use or reliance upon the information and material provided herein. We are unable to provide any

This book was written by me and I am not a professional writer. Because of this there may be some errors of grammar, punctuation and some other areas that could be improved. If you see any mistakes or have any suggestions for improvement, please email me at addictionhacks1@gmail.com and let me know about them, Thank You!

ACKNOWLEDGEMENT

There have been countless people on my journey who've inspired, taught and influenced me in more ways than I can count. From the beginning of my journey I had an insatiable need to learn, use what I've learned and then to teach. Throughout my life, there were lessons to be learned and my teachers appeared. I want to thank every one of those who took the time to guide and influence me.

I could add countless names to this acknowledgment and all that would prove is that I was blessed to work with some of the best teachers in the world. But this book is about you, not me.

Thank you to each and every one of you who have helped me along the way. Your knowledge, wisdom, caring and compassion, for me and others is greatly appreciated. You know who you are as I have thanked each and every one of you individually.

FOREWARD

YES, THERE IS A BETTER WAY!

By Dr. Steven Roth DMD, CHT, CMT

Drug overdoses have become the leading cause of death of Americans under the age of 50; two-thirds of these deaths are from opioids. In fact, this crisis is decreasing the overall life expectancy of Americans. The problem is not going away and the relapse rate of drug addicts is over 70%.

I've been a practicing dentist for over 30 years, a life coach, a Medical Hypnotherapist using the modalities of cognitive behavioral therapy, Hypnotherapy, and Neuro-linguistic programming for over a decade. I've wondered when a new protocol for preventing the addict from falling back into relapse would be developed because the current way is not working.

Well, there is a better way to change and change quickly. For too long addiction therapy took countless sessions, immense self-control and the support system that relied on others. This book, changes that pattern and countless lives as well by using these simple steps to become "drug-free". Why wait?

William Nixon's Addiction-Hack protocol addresses many of the issues missed by many other programs. He uses a tough-love approach helping the client to realize the results of their choices in the past, the possible consequences if they were to continue making the same poor choices and most importantly, he helps his clients realize their full potential, and that they are capable of accomplishing everything they put their mind to.

Henry Ford; visionary, innovator and founder of the Ford Motor Company once said: "Whether you think you can or think you can't, you're right!" From my experience, believing you don't have the ability to change and low self-worth is a common denominator and characteristic of the addict, Bill addresses this wonderfully with his protocol.

It was 2007 when I met Bill Nixon at the International Association of Counselors and Therapist (I.A.C.T.) conference in Florida. From that first meeting until today some 14 years later I've come to know Bill as honest, genuine and caring. Those same qualities, plus his understanding of addictions have led him to some major breakthroughs in the treatment of addictions. His personal challenges could have held him back, but using the same techniques in the book they actually propelled him forward. I witnessed firsthand his remarkable change.

I know a lady that called him for help one day. They were hundreds of miles away from each other and both driving at the time. They both pulled their cars over; Bill guided her through a quick process. 11 years later she has not needed any reinforcement. Yes, this book covers the same steps to change. You too can be one of the many success stories Bill will share. So what are you waiting for? NOW is a great time to start and have the wonderful life you deserve!

For too long counselors therapist and doctors assumed it takes years of therapy to change. This book debunks that theory. Bill's extensive training and his own struggles have given him an insight few possess. He is recognized as an internationally certified instructor, teacher, and mentor (Board Certified). Now, through this book, he can be your coach, mentor, and friend. Read and use the technique in this book and change is inevitable.

Dr. Steven Roth DMD, CHT, CMT.

Founder of Elite Hypnotherapy- Medical Hypnosis

Www.elitehypno.com

Founder of the G.I.F.T. Program

www.receiveyourgift.com

TABLE OF CONTENTS

WHAT THIS BOOK IS ABOUT

AND, WHAT THIS BOOK IS NOT ABOUT

Hi my name is William Nixon…

Before you begin reading this book let me give you a clear picture of what this book is about and more importantly what it's not about.

This book is NOT a book that you read, and then miraculously you're changed. At the same time if you read this book, do the exercises with emotions then change is inevitable.

This book is NOT about psychobabble but, it is a practical step-by-step process to change. What is it you'd like to change? Would you like freedom from drugs or alcohol addictions, stop eating sugar or some other "habit" that is robbing you of some part of your life?

This book is NOT about placing blame, finding fault or criticizing those of us (me included) who have, now or in the past dealt with addictions.

This book is about change. Change happens in an instant. That may sound like a bold statement, but it's one, as you begin to read this book you will totally understand. This book is a step-by-step manual for your mind.

This book is about understanding the whys of what we do and don't do. If you understand your "human needs", notice I said needs, not wants you'll know how to change, and make it permanent.

I highly recommend you read this book cover to cover before beginning, what will be a life-changing experience. I've also written comprehensive workbooks that help streamline the process and a series of instructional audios that are to be used with the workbooks. Should you have any questions feel free to email me at addictionhacks1@gmail.com

WHY THIS BOOK?

The reason I do this is, it gives me great pleasure to help people. I have been blessed by so many experiences and worked with some of the greatest teachers. Not sharing my knowledge would be ultimate pain and in my opinion a sin. I've spent a great deal of money and time going to seminars, workshops, retreats and other events to learn to live at the highest levels that I could, and in the process I learned how to help others. I have helped and seen massive changes in people who have used these techniques. At the same time I've seen countless and useless therapies that simply failed the person. But they did not fail the therapist, doctors or the treatment centers because, they made massive amounts of money, sadly they had little to no results. A lot of therapists do a lot of good. I've worked with psychologists, psychiatrists and other mental health professionals, all of which have their place.

But, I was interested in immediate results....

Why did some people change quickly and others take 60 or 70 sessions, only to find that the change was just mediocre?

Why did some people go to rehab multiple times with little or no change?

I wanted to know the answers, so my search began.

In the mid-80s, I'm dating myself now, LOL; I worked with a gentleman who at the time was called a forensic hypnotist. His job was to help people remember events from the past. The police would seek his assistance to help someone remember a license plate number of a car they had witnessed in an accident or something similar. He taught me about the conscious and the subconscious mind and how I could change myself and my bad habits without tremendous effort. In the early 90s I got serious and began getting formal training by attending seminars, schools, and workshops. At one point in my life I put a deposit down to purchase a private jet for my leisure activity. I went from incredibly poor financially to fairly well-off. At that time, I had a business that was the target of a "hostile takeover" and pretty much lost everything except my ability to think and feel, and the knowledge that I had gained.

The techniques I now teach helped me rebound without the scars of the past. Having a business was something I enjoyed. But as it came time to retire, I realized I would not be happy golfing every day, going out to dinner every night and traveling endlessly for entertainment. I needed to give back and that is why you're on my website, reading this book or listing to the audio book. The stories I can tell you, the people I've helped are not only uplifting for them, their families, but for me as well. Some of the people I have worked with are the most caring, kind and compassionate people I know. When I leave this earth I will do so knowing that I've helped many people live the life that they could only dream of. If you had a gift, wouldn't it give you more pleasure to share it, rather than to keep it? For me it's about the giving.

I would like to think in some way, I'm going to change the world and make it a better place. I don't think that's unreasonable and in fact I think it's practical.

Watching people grow to become the person that they could and should be is one of the greatest gifts of life. I am in a place in my life now that most people can only dream of. I have a wife who I adore, and a family who I deeply love. My needs are met financially and spiritually, yet I still need more.

I need to contribute. I need to help people who have been less fortunate than me or have never been exposed to the methods of change that this book offers. While I am writing this book, I am working with two very competent and compassionate individuals because there are more people in this world than I can possibly help. Dr. Steven Roth from Miami, Florida and Amy Emmi from Fort Myers, Florida, both of these individuals have extensive training in Hypnotherapy, and Neuro-linguistic programming. If they were to give out degrees for competence, these two would be "Ultra PhD's" in results. I've work with others along the way, but these two are the core of my team.

When you have incredible success, as I know you will, I would love to hear from you. Please email me at addictionhacks1@gmail.com about your successes.

My best to you,

Bill

DISEASE

OR, AS I LIKE TO CALL IT, DIS-EASE

This very small chapter may not be welcomed by the medical community, whose job, along with the drug companies is to classify, quantify and label people. Sometimes for profit, and other times for clarification! I will agree there are some diseases that actually do exist, polio, malaria and cancer all come to mind. What doesn't come to mind are the terms and labels for people who, for whatever reason make bad choices. No blame here, but they continue to make bad choices, as we all have done from time to time.

The medical community uses labels for people who over drink alcohol, they call them alcoholics. People who do drugs, whether it is prescribed by the physicians or not, these people are called drug addicts. What about people that over indulge in food, are they called food addicts? What about people who crave sugar, are they sugar addicts? Maybe we should classify them as carbo addicts? The list goes on and on, as do the labels.

There are some advantages to being labeled and many disadvantages. Let's talk about some of the advantages. Let's say you've been labeled an alcoholic. Great, not so great.... but at least you now have a reason why you drink too much and it's not your fault! Really, whose fault is it?

What if you're labeled a drug addict? So, is it okay to destroy your life and everyone else's around you because, it's not your fault? What I'm simply saying here is that you may be acting like an alcoholic or an addict, but that *is not* who you are! Here's the point and this one is BIG, if you say you're a drug addict, marijuana addict, alcoholic, food addict, and then in your own mind, you are one.

At this time in your life you may have an addictive personality and rightfully so. In the chapter, pain/pleasure you'll understand why you have an addictive personality and that is not your fault! What should be your fault is choosing to not change, after learning how to change quickly. If you learn why, and you choose not to change, that is your fault.

I often wonder if Albert Einstein were in school today, what he would have been labeled. What would have happened if Einstein believed the teachers or doctors? Would he have given up and not pursued his mathematics? Would he be labeled ADHD or some other crazy label?

If the doctors and drug companies can label it, there's profit to be made. From 2015 to 2019 the cost of addictions has doubled and it's not going away.

Substance abuse costs our Nation over $600 billion annually and with proper treatment we can help reduce these costs. Drug addiction treatment has been shown to reduce associated health and social costs by far more than the cost of the treatment itself. Treatment is also much less expensive than its alternatives, such as incarcerating addicted persons.

For example, the average cost for one full year of methadone maintenance treatment is approximately $4,700 per patient, whereas one full year of imprisonment costs approximately $24,000 per person.

https://www.drugabuse.gov/publications/principles-drug-addiction-treatment-research-based-guide-third-edition/frequently-asked-questions/drug-addiction-treatment-worth-its-cost

Americans spend an estimated $276 billion every year drinking, smoking and taking drugs, according to a recent analysis. To give that huge figure some perspective, that's more than the federal government spent in 2015 on education and veterans' benefits combined. I read a report recently that that number was well over $300 billion in 2017 and climbing.

https://www.aol.com/article/finance/2016/09/30/drug-and-alcohol-addiction-costs-americans-276-billion-a-year/21483951/

RESPONSIBILITY

Whose responsibility is it to control your life? Is it other people, the government including social services, the media or you? The word responsibility can be thought of as the ability to respond. Unlike most animals, humans have the ability to respond rather than react. At our core we will react, but for the most part we can respond.

Time and time again I've seen people blame others for their situations. We are responsible for ourselves. We can blame the past for who we are, as long as we do not take responsibility for ourselves.

For the most part, people have not been taught how to truly think and change and therefore have not taken the action to make the changes necessary in their life. I will not tell you that past experiences don't affect us, they do. Tony Robbins says "the past does not define the future" in other words the past is the past and the future is what you make of it.

This book is written in a way to help you take responsibility and be **assured** of the results in advance. Yes, you can make changes now that will dramatically improve and change your future, if you choose to change. If you make the choice, this book will help you make it a reality and put you on a path to success however you define it.

For some people success would be to stop drinking, to others quit smoking, some want to lose those excess pounds and for others stop doing drugs. Some may want $1 million or $5 million in their bank account. We are all different and what I'm doing is giving you the directions and the map on how to get to your destination.

But first, you must take responsibility. What does that mean? It simply means you make the distinction and the decision that you can and will change. At this time, you do not have to know how; you simply have to know that you will change. Up until this time, chances are you've never been told or instructed on how to change.

Sure, if you've been an alcoholic, some people will tell you just don't drink. That sounds simple, but yet without knowing why you drink, chances are you will continue to drink. For now, I only want you to make one decision. You must decide to change whatever behavior you want to change immediately.

It is highly recommended that you make only one change at this time to prove to yourself how simple it can be. You do not have to change the most complex, difficult or challenging behavior at this time, but I would recommend you also don't choose something so simple, such as I will no longer chew gum at work. Make it real, make it important, and make it something that can make a major impact on your life today.

As you go through this book you will see some worksheets that you can use to begin the process. But for now, simply choose a behavior that you feel you <u>need</u> to change. The worksheet "Why I Must Change" is useful but only after you read the chapter on "Why I Must Change".

THE BASICS OF FAST AND PREMANENT CHANGE

It wasn't long ago, I was asked if I could do a presentation to a group of professionals that included; doctors, psychologists, dentists and hypnotherapist, most of who have had extensive training in the field of addictions. I was then asked if I could do it in seven minutes, I laughed, accepted the challenge and wrote this book summary as a handout.

This book summary explains how we are programmed from birth, and how and why we do what we do. Over 97% of what we do is subconscious or as I like to say "non-thinking, thinking". It's now been proven that we are able and capable to control some of our subconscious mind. There are a few basic concepts or as I like to call them truths, that are helpful to know.

Truth # One

There are six human needs that all humans, regardless of where they are from, have at the core of their being. Whether, they are the most sophisticated people in the world, or tribes in the deepest parts of the Amazon Basin who have yet to be discovered. <u>All human beings have the same six needs.</u> Notice I said needs, not wants. These six human needs are certainty, variety, significance, love/connection, growth and contribution.

Truth # Two

If you know, understand and use these truths, You Can Change! In fact, by using the process outlined in this book, change is virtually guaranteed. You can change the vast majority of your life and your future. Imagine being able to control your mind to a point that the same power that keeps you addicted, now becomes stronger to repel you away from your addiction.

You know how the addiction feels, the "feelings and cravings" it draws you in, and you feel helpless in its power? Imagine for a second that that same power now pushes you away from the drug more powerfully. Your addiction would be history. I'll show you how to control the cravings and stop the unwanted behavior without the normal withdrawal pain or behaviors and have it done almost automatically.

Truth # Three

We are born and hardwired to avoid pain and death. Pain, as our mind sees it is anything that causes us discomfort. In our deepest reptilian mind, all pain is thought to hurt us and thus to be avoided. Examples of these are physical pain, humiliation, embarrassment, feelings of failure, fear of success, fear of death, fear of loss such as love, money and pride. Avoiding pain and discomfort is our mind's way to prevent us from death. As human beings, an early or premature death would've been certain if it wasn't for the fight/flight response. The problem is we no longer have dinosaurs chasing us, yet, our mind doesn't know that. By using this power to its advantage, we can make changes almost instantly.

Truth # Four

We are also programmed to seek pleasure. This is nowhere near as strong as the need to avoid pain but, it is one of our needs and thus we can use it to our advantage. Pleasure comes in many ways for instance love, friendships, accomplishments, minor and major successes and yes food, drugs and alcohol.

At this time, if you're an addict, the drug you seek can make you feel both pleasure and at the same time pain. But at the very moment you give into your addiction, you are seeking pleasure to <u>avoid pain</u>!

So why do most addicts continue down the spiraling path of destruction? It's because they are avoiding the pain of detox, rehabilitation, humiliation, failure and countless other reasons. They are only looking for instant pleasure. The very moment they make that decision they are trying to avoid the pain and seek pleasure. Quite often at that very moment, the mind is deciding which is "least painful". If the person continues the drug of choice they are fulfilling their need to avoid pain. But, if you deny the urge to use drugs, consume alcohol or over indulge in food you will feel the pain immediately, so your brain thinks. So pain drives the decision whether it's real or imagined. If you think about it, pain and fear are what stops you for living a better life.

Pain is real. Our subconscious perceives pain as the ultimate enemy and if we seek and continue with this undesired pleasure of our addiction we will avoid this pain throughout our lives. Now understand this, it is our mind that wants to avoid pain at any cost, quitting, going to rehab, detox these all can cause extreme pain, as our mind sees it. Your subconscious mind wants to avoid pain and thus you continue your addiction.

How to use this knowledge? This may sound so simple, yet it's so powerful. You need to reprogram or simply re-think who you are. How do I do that you might ask? First you have to make a commitment to follow through the process and know your outcome in advance; yes, I said, know you're outcome in advance or at the minimum, imagine it and begin to believe it. This does not say hope for your outcome, KNOW YOUR OUTCOME in advance.

Just know and trust me that you will succeed by following the steps in this book.

THE PROCESS OF RECOVERY

The process that we use is designed to strengthen your subconscious mind. That is the part of the mind that controls most of your functions, for example the blinking of your eyes, keeping your temperature at 98.6F, keeping your balance, your heart beating and thousands of other processes. All of which you don't think about consciously.

It's been said that if the subconscious mind was the size of a huge covered football stadium, than your conscious mind would be the size of a golf ball. Which do you think has the most power? The subconscious mind has the most power by thousands of times. That's why working with the subconscious mind using visual, auditory, guided visualizations and the pain/pleasure connection, gets results fast.

Addictive behaviors are generally a subconscious program that prevents you from pain or harm. Your addiction is a **learned addiction** that can be **unlearned**. To start and maintain your addiction you had to learn it! My team and I all have extensive training and spectacular results that will help you eliminate the addictions quickly, thus total recovery.

The use of guided visualizations is how the mind works and thinks and helps to create a future that your brain, at the subconscious level wants you to have. The patterns of addiction can be replaced by patterns of recovery and fulfillment. Please pay special attention to this next sentence, as it will help you understand where you are, as well is where you are going.

The strongest force in the human race, is the need to remain consistent, with who you think you are!

Think about this for a moment, many people who have been released from rehab centers continue to think that they are addicts, alcoholics and drug users. Seriously! It's sad to think that they've sought help by checking into rehab only to be released and told that they hadn't changed they were still an addict. Desperate to get help they contacted me and actually admitted to me that the rehab centers labeled them that they were still addicts, alcoholics and drug users, REALLY!!! *No wonder they didn't change!* As humans our needs are to remain consistent with who we think we are. These people were released believing that they were still addicts, alcoholics, and drug users, so guess what? They still were in "their own minds" addicts. Using sheer willpower is the most difficult way to change. Real change must occur within the mind, the subconscious mind.

What if the subconscious mind at the deepest level felt, and knew that the drugs, alcohol, opioids etc. we're going to cause great pain and even death? Would you be driven toward or away from the substance of choice? Of course the answer is away from the substance, away from the pain. On the other hand, what if having an incredible life, free of addiction and getting back your freedom and health were part of the process;

17

do you think your mind would be driven towards that outcome? You bet it would!

So this process can be broken down into simple steps. Number one is to determine and understand what the pain of your addiction is costing you and others around you <u>now</u> and in your <u>future</u>. When you at your deepest level understand the impact in terms of your health, your family, your friends, your job, money and your life, change can and will begin. Our goal is to help you discover your "hot buttons" for change.

The next step is to determine the pleasure you will receive, the benefits you will gain, when you are no longer addicted. Again, <u>we will do more to avoid pain than to seek pleasure.</u> But, when we use both pain and pleasure the force is unequaled.

I have worked with extreme marijuana addicts, alcoholics, opioid dependent drug abusers, food abusers and many others who have had addictions. In almost every case, the reason they stayed addicted was because the <u>pain of quitting</u> seemed unbearable. Think about that last statement, in their mind they believed that the pain to quit was so great that they would rather continue using drugs knowing that eventually, it would destroy them. I will tell you now that if you follow this process to quit it will not be that painful. It will be very uncomfortable, but not in a physical way.

The reason they didn't change, was because they still believed they were addicts! Most likely you weren't born an addict but, sadly some adults were born addicted to drugs but that wasn't by their choice. You're a person who's doing addictive things, and that's not who you are, it's only who you think you are.

Just a side note:

I met with a man who just got out of detox and rehab for OxyContin; he explained to me that even though he was "clean" in his mind he was still an addict. His self-image and his self-esteem was that of an addict. He knew he needed to change but he also knew that his will power wasn't going to be enough!

The final part of our process is what we call reinforcement. We reinforce the pleasure of your new behaviors and lifestyle. The reinforcement process can be described as simply writing down, feeling and visualizing the changes you've made, and the changes that will occur in your future. Depending on the person we sometimes will make a recording that will guide you through this positive reinforcement. Other people who have read this book, made their own recordings. Email me and I will send you an outline on how to do this; when emailing me please add the following to the subject line: "Recording Reinforcement".

I hired a PhD who is a professor in psychology who specializes in addiction, to help me develop a test to determine learning and thinking styles. The test is called V.A.K., which stands for Visual, Auditory and Kinesthetic. We also determine how to use your "mind's eye". This is also known as NLP which is short for Neuro–Linguistic Programming. This is how our mind processes what we see, what we hear, how we feel, all this takes place in your mind. This may sound complicated and to some it is, but using this knowledge helps us, help you at the deepest level. When we produce audio sessions for some of our clients we use the V.A.K. test to guarantee results.

My family personally experienced the consequences of drug addictions when a relative of mine confessed that he was addicted to OxyContin. I know firsthand how addictions destroy people's lives, those who love them and the people they come in contact with. He followed the process exactly as I've outlined it above and to this day it's been over five years and he has not touched the former drug of choice.

Not long after he quit he was visiting at a friend's home when someone at the house offered him some drugs he became so angry that he told that person, if you ever do that again you will face severe consequences. He immediately left the house and swore he'd never go back. That's positive change! Think about that, what he was addicted to has created such anger and pain in his mind, that he swore he'd never use again.

So if it seems that I'm a little fanatical, it's because I am. I want for you nothing less, than to give you back the life you were meant to live. To help you remove the chains of addiction and open your eyes to the possibilities of a new healthy life. When you stop the addictive behavior, it can create a vacuum in your life, to gravitate towards good behaviors and to replace the old ones.

This process is a very personal process to us and of course, it is to you as well. Things like walking, exercising, going to the gym, reading books even going back to school are some of the things that I've seen clients do. In MA (Marijuana Anonymous), AA (Alcoholics Anonymous) and NA (Narcotics Anonymous) they say: "Change your playgrounds and playthings." To paraphrase this, change the places you go, the people you hang out with.

Let's think of it this way, if you take a bath in rose milk, you will get out and smell like a rose. If you walk through a cow pasture and step in cow shit, you will smell like cow shit. Choose the path in life you want to walk and the people you want to walk with.

PAIN PLEASURE CONNECTION

The pain/pleasure connection as it relates to our lives as human beings is to avoid pain and seek pleasure. Have your every wondered why, it because we are hardwired to avoid pain and seek pleasure. This is a survival mechanism that generally controls us, and not us controlling these behaviors, until now!

In this simple yet profound chapter you'll understand what controls us at our deepest levels and how we can control our outcomes. From the moment we are born we will try to avoid pain.

What is pain? I'm not talking about physical pain although we want to avoid that as well, I'm talking about *emotional pain*; things such as rejection, embarrassment, failure, loneliness and so many other emotional feelings that cause pain. Although we are wired to avoid pain at the deepest depths of our soul, this can be attributed to the feeling of certain death I know this sounds overdramatic, but it's not.

Animals, which we are, instinctually try to avoid pain and death, as this is part of our survival mechanism. But the part of our brain that helps us survive cannot tell the difference between the different types of "emotional pain" present or future. It only knows to avoid pain.

Here's a very basic example of emotional pain; there's someone who you are very attracted to, oh how you would love to ask them out on a date. This person could possibly be a potential life partner, but you don't ask because the pain of rejection is so powerful. Asking someone out takes courage but in a state of hopelessness you become scared, and scared of rejection and the devastating fact that rejection causes great pain. It is very interesting that our brain doesn't really see the difference between this and falling off a cliff or being hunted by a dinosaur. But now that you think about it, it certainly isn't life or death but to our brain, it is all pain!

Now what if we introduced pleasure as part of this process? What if instead of seeing the possibility of being rejected, you see the possibility of dating someone who you are extremely attracted to. If in your mind you can make the distinction that asking this person out on a date could be ultimate pleasure, that could be more powerful than a simple rejection.

Again we are <u>wired</u> to avoid pain and seek pleasure, yet, the more powerful of the two is avoiding pain. <u>We will do far more to avoid pain than to seek pleasure.</u> As another very simple example, why would someone continue doing destructive things to their body instead of quitting alcohol or drugs or overeating? Because they associate so much more pain to quitting than they do to the pleasure of being sober and healthy. I will repeat this sentence because it is so important; *<u>they associate more pain to quitting than they do to the pleasure of being sober and healthy</u>*.

This might seem crazy at first but it is extremely powerful. We will do more to avoid pain than seek pleasure.

Imagine for a second that by using drugs, drinking alcohol overindulging in foods and sugar, only to find yourself in undeniable pain and that by NOT using these addictive devices you could seek incredible pleasure, what would you do? You would stop wouldn't you? Stop the pain!

In this book you will have the tools to make this incredibly powerful hardwired decision; you're empowered, you have control and you are your own boss. You CAN control your own destiny with a powerful mind.

WHO LABELED YOU?

Every one of us carries around a self-image that we either created for ourselves or was given to us by someone else, usually an authority figure.

Our parents, teachers and friends have all made comments which at the time seemed harmless, yet they could be what's defining us right now. The words, if we accept them, such as stupid, smart, brilliant, fat, skinny, moron can define our ability to learn and think. Other words and phrases such as, you're a star athlete, you're too slow, you're very strong, you're a weakling, you're too fat etc. all have defined us, whether we like it or not. But, the reality is *we* can change those labels, to what we want them to be. The reality is you've probably let other people define you, until now.

The methods used in this book will dramatically change who you think you are, to whom you actually want to be. If you feel you are an addict, alcoholic, slow learner, druggie, fat, skinny or whatever, this book will give you the blueprint to change, and to change ***NOW***!

I have seen it time and time again that change happens in an instant. But the only one that can make that decision is you. Interestingly, the word "decision" comes from the Latin word to "cut off from". So what are you waiting for, you are someone other than that label, so once you recognize that this label doesn't' fit any longer the change immediately begins. It's time to accept a new label, a new identity; a new life, the one you want.

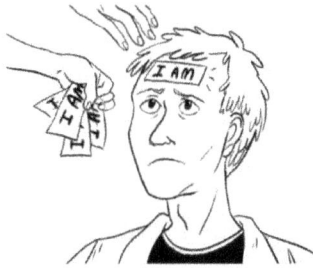

How did you get that label that you've accepted?

Generally it happens when an authority figure such as a teacher, a parent or one of your peers be littles you or criticizes you by calling you names and telling you that you are something less than perfect. Words like dumb, stupid, ignorant, fat can all be labels that are hurtful and ingrained in our brain. At that instant, and I mean instantly, when it was said, "if in your mind" you agreed with it, you accepted the label! Yes it happens instantly and without your knowledge.

My job is to help you change who you think you are at this very moment, to who you want to be, your true self. Let's think of it this way if you say you're an alcoholic, you are! It's that simple. I remember years ago I kept telling myself I'm not a good speller and I believed that fully.

At the time I had several secretaries who marveled at how I could write such beautiful letters and technical papers, yet my spelling was atrocious. One day I was thinking about my spelling, if I could read a book and find tons of misspelled words, how could I do that if I couldn't spell? At that very instant I decided that I was a good speller but, I was not taking the time when I wrote papers or letters to spell correctly. Over the next two months I would write letters and give these to my secretaries to be typed. A month passed and my secretaries were betting among themselves, how did my spelling improve? They thought maybe I was using a computer, a dictionary or at the time one of those little pocket electronic spellcheckers.

They came to my office because it intrigued them to the point that they just had to know. When they asked me, I explained to them that I simply just took more time because I knew I was a good speller. They laughed and I proceeded to explain that I could read books and see words that were misspelled, including some of their work!

How could I do that if I couldn't spell well? I explained that I changed my self-image to that of a great speller, who for the most part didn't take time to spell correctly. Whose label had I accepted for over 45 years ago? I imagine it went back to elementary school when I was in the "bluebird" reading group. We were the ones who didn't read well and couldn't spell!

So who gave you the label that you accepted? To give you an example of how I've used this process myself; I routinely have an annual physical checkup, but my recent visit to the doctors proved differently, I was diagnosed as a diabetic. I was shocked and immediately told the doctor, NO, I wasn't. I would not accept his diabetic labeling of me and I wanted my brain to know that. A year later I met with my new doctor and we went over my blood results for the last three months, he said, "Why were you labeled a diabetic?" I laughed and said I guess it was a mistake.

Now I'm not saying you can do that if you're a true diabetic, but if I had accepted the label and continued to eat the wrong foods and stop exercising, guess what? I not only would've accepted the label but I would've definitely become a true diabetic.

I want you to know from the bottom of my heart; change is not only possible, it's practical. It's a lot easier than living with the pain and discomfort of accepting someone else's judgment about who you are.

*"The strongest force in the human race is the **need** to remain consistent with who we think we are".*

Had I, for one second and that's all it would've taken, one second accepted the doctors label and agreed mentally that I was a diabetic I would be one now. I may have been border-line, but I'm not anymore. For the record, I'm not telling you that just thinking you don't have a medical condition changes your condition, I'm just saying not all labels are accurate and change is possible.

This is not positive thinking; this is thinking positively about who you really are. My biggest rewards have been coaching some incredible people. Most importantly, it's when I've been able to teach them how to make changes for themselves and not need any more help from me.

When I first started out with my current coach, we worked several times a week together to make the changes I desired. It's been years now since that first meeting and to this day I appreciate all the work that he put me through. We still work together a few times a year. Yes, I still have a coach! My job is to teach you to fish, so you can feed yourself for a lifetime, not fish for you and feed you for one day.

WHAT STOPS YOU?

We are wired to avoid pain sometimes disguised as fear. Our brain at the subconscious level is wired for fear and pain. It is a survival mechanism that helps ensure our species will continue. Once we get a little older we instinctively begin to fear things that could hurt us. I don't know anyone who could go on top of a twenty story building, walk to the very edge looking down and wouldn't have some fear. But the fear we are talking about today is emotional fear and pain.

You hear all the time about fear of failure, fear of success, but what about the fear of not being good enough? What about being embarrassed is that also a fear? **Yes**, fear is emotional and because of that it is an incredibly powerful emotion to use for change.

The problem and the solution is that our subconscious mind can't tell the difference between imagined fear and real fear. When you're in school and the teacher calls on you to answer a question, how did you react? Did you want to escape, did you freeze or did you know the answer and not have any emotional response? If you got the answer wrong, you could have felt humiliation or rejection, and that's pain.

Our brain recognizes pain and fear as death and wants to avoid it at all cost. The same for peer groups, when we were younger or even now they can be both good and destructive. Either way your brain wants to avoid the negative and painful emotions and escape. If you have been bullied, it could still be with you years later and most likely they are still painful memories.

It's unlikely that the majority of our fear is warranted in today's society. We no longer have dinosaurs or wildlife chasing us for their afternoon lunch, yet that part of our mind still functions as if we are being chased. Fear has an acronym that is useful to remember, "False Evidence Appearing Real".

When we think of real change, our mind will look back at times we tried to change and didn't. It may have been we didn't know how, but our mind will remember the failure of not being able to change. That failure could be thought of as embarrassment or you're "just not good enough" and that is pain, and pain causes us fear, all to be avoided like death.

So, what can we do? Do we stop doing anything that causes us any pain or discomfort? Well, we are wired that way, but by using the pain/pleasure method, we basically force our brain to feel the pain and the fear, because consciously we know the outcome will be pleasurable and good for us.

Have you heard the saying do what you fear most and the fear will disappear? It's a very true statement and the more you exercise your ability to face the fear, the easier it becomes. I'm not saying that you should go out into the wild and look for grizzly bears to chase you, or walk to the edge of a building to look down. What I'm saying is when it comes to our emotional well-being facing fear and pain is the fastest way to change.

One last little thought about fear and pain. What if you don't face the fear and the pain in your life right now? Will things change in the next week, month, year or ten years? If you continue on the same track, doing the same things in your life will it get better, worse or stay the same? The definition of insanity is "doing the same thing over and over again and expecting different results".

It's time to make a change and we are here to help you.

THE PAST

I s the past holding you back? From my observation I would say 99.9% of the population is held back by their past. The stories we tell ourselves, the movies we play in our heads, and the fears caused by past embarrassments or failures have held us back from our true potential. I could make this chapter a book if I chose to, but then, why would I help you live in the past? That would truly be a dis-service to you and everyone in your world.

For a moment I would like you to imagine driving a car. Do this simple exercise. Get into your imaginary car and begin to drive down the road, making a few turns, stopping at traffic lights, stopping at stop signs, speeding towards the highway of your future. Now drive onto a major highway/freeway at normal speeds. The road begins to curve and go up and down hills for many miles. How did you do? Were you able to navigate safely? Sure you were you were looking ahead. Now let's take the same scenario and the same drive. The only difference this time is I want you to drive by looking only in your rearview mirror! How far do you think you'll make it on this drive? The reality is we tend to drive our lives by constantly looking in the rearview mirror of our past. It's nice to know where we've been, but it's not helpful when you're trying to make it to a destination, setting a goal or to change a behavior that's destroying you and others around you.

Whenever you think of your past, think about driving your car using only the rearview mirror, and know that you're going to crash. Now look forward and begin to drive your life into the future that you envisioned.

GETTING READY FOR FREEDOM

Before you begin this part of the process it is recommended that your body be detoxed for at least 24 hours. For drug and alcohol or any addictions I recommend contacting a physician and following their recommendation for detoxing. You may be surprised to find out how much clearer your mind will be after your substance of choice is out of your blood system. Now, if you have detoxed, the following is a guideline to set you free. The book Addiction-Hacks goes into great detail as do some of my blogs. But if you feel you're ready, this is the basic outline.

First get prepared. Pick a time and safe and quiet place to work. Pick a place to work that you won't be disturbed or disturb others because during this process you will be writing, thinking, crying, and laughing. You will need a notebook or blank paper, and pen or pencil.

This is actually very easy to do but the vast majority of people; teachers, college professors and even psychiatrist and psychologist don't know how to explain this.

Begin by thinking.

So, here it goes Thinking 101. You're going to ask yourself a question; and answer the question. That's thinking! But why ask questions? "Aha, now you're thinking!"

The reason to ask questions is so you control the question and thus the answer. A word of caution here, don't just get the answer, feel the emotion of the answer. Here's an example of a question; why does everything go wrong in my life? The answer pre-supposes that everything goes wrong and your brain will search your mind to find the answer, thus proving that everything does go wrong.

Now ask this question. What has gone right in my life? Again, your mind will find what has gone right in your life. What am I good at in my life? Some people answer that with "I'm not good at anything!" If you think that way, think again. If you're reading this, you may not think you're good at something, but you're good enough to read this, and many people can't read!

Begin by thinking and asking questions that make you feel better about yourself.

Some examples I've used with my clients and myself are as follows: Who loves me? Who likes me? Who do I love? Who do I like? Who could I like? Who could I love? Who could like me? Who could love me? What's great in my life? What could be great in my life? Once you've asked yourself these questions, try to get at least 20 answers for each one.

Now, come up with 20 great questions! What am I good at or could be good at? What accomplishments have I made in my life? What were positive things said about me by my family, friends, coworkers, bosses teachers? Again, try to get at least 20 answers to each question, think hard the best answers are usually the last few.

The workbooks contain great questions to help with this part of the process. You need to be honest here. We are taught from a young age to be modest and during this exercise that would be useless. Be honest, many people have said many good things about you and it's time to recognize them and accept them.

The second step is the reverse and is painful. Knowing that we want to avoid pain at all cost, this will take a conscious decision to move forward. If you cause enough pain in your mind about your current addiction and behavior, your mind will help you change quickly.

This step is not going to be easy you need to ask questions that will cause you emotional pain and discomfort. No, let's skip the discomfort and go straight to pain. The more emotional pain you feel during this process, the greater the results.

When you're ready, sit down with your paper and pencil and asked the tough questions. Tough questions like: Who have I hurt? What pain have I caused each and every one of them? Continuing this addiction will not only destroy me but also others around me those that care for me. You'll have to dig deep here and **feel** the pain of both you and the other people you are hurting.

Ask this question, if I don't change, what will happen in thirty days from now, where will I be, and who will I be with? Now the same question for sixty days, then six months and then one year. What will your life look like if you are continuing on this cycle of despair and addiction?

If you have any questions or need a little help here, feel free to email me at addictionhacks1@gmail.com this part of the process should take 30 to 60 minutes to complete.

When I first did this process I felt the intense pain, I cried, I began to shake and wanted to puke. My head hurt, my gut hurt and I felt absolutely horrible. The good news is it worked. This isn't where it ended it was only the beginning but it did end the pain. After spending an hour or so asking and answering questions that caused me intense emotional pain, I stood up and literally shook off the bad feelings. I drank water, walked around and even looked in a mirror I had a big gigantic silly smile on my face, and I knew I had changed!

The next step is to ask the opposite type of question. Assuming that you're going to leave your addiction behind during this process, begin by asking empowering questions and FEEL the answers. Why is my life getting better day by day? How much better will I feel? What is my life going to look like in thirty days, ninety days or six months? What will my life be like in one year, five years or even ten years from now because I'm free of any addictions? Ask questions like who loves me? Who will be proud of me? By the way, first one on that list should be YOU!

I realize this is the extremely short version of the process and as such you don't get all the "meat and potatoes" of the book. You can go to my blog and see more details and videos about how this is done. I will tell you this; this process has changed thousands of people's lives, quickly! My wish for you is that you have the greatest life you dream of, whatever that may be for you!

SUCCESS STORIES

I n the late 1990's a man who I knew briefly asked me if I
could help him with his addictions. His name was Kenny,
and he was an extreme alcoholic, drug user and homeless.
At first I thought he was kidding and I said "you want to
change?" And he said yes, this is when the process began.

This is his story. He was a football player, wide receiver
for The University of Miami, Florida and in the summer of his
junior year, his life changed forever. During football practice
he was tackled from the side and the resulting injury was one
that he would never fully recover from. At the time of the
accident the school terminated his scholarship, even though it
was no fault of his own.

Several weeks later he was walking on campus when two
men approached him in dark suits introducing themselves as
recruiters for the government. The University of Miami is
located in the deep south of the United States where it is very
hot and muggy. These recruiters offered him a job working for
a government agency, and if he accepted they would pay for
the rest of his education at any school he wanted. He accepted

the position with the government and went on to get his Degree in Finance and Economics from Temple University, Florida.

Kenny was highly intelligent, yet became an alcoholic and drug user. After graduation he went to work in what he describes as covert operations. He said he witnessed things that no one should ever see. In order to overcome things that he had witnessed, he turned to alcohol to avoid pain and seek pleasure. Kenny had such an incredible education, a pension plan, and a promising future, but he eventually lost everything.

Who he had been and what he had done were memories, and quite often they were bad memories. He knew he needed to change and if he didn't, he would stay homeless, a drunk and probably dead within a few years.

This is where my expertise came in. He asked me for help and I agreed but, not at first.

I told him to make a list of what he wanted to change, and why? He came back to me with this little list that was almost embarrassing. His list had insignificant reasons to change. Things like, I will feel better but not great, I can make enough money to rent a room. You get the idea these items were non-emotional things to change. I told him he might like to change, but deep down inside he wasn't ready, nor did he really **need** to change

It took Kenny about three months to come to me with a list that made sense. We sat down and discussed the massive amounts of pain he had caused himself and others including his family. We talked about his health and how in a few years he would be dead. We talked about some of his family, former coworkers, football friends from the past and how this hurt them as well. We also talked about the fact he had lost all of his friends from the past.

This went on for several days as he was updating and changing his list. About a week later he came to me with a list that was three pages long of why he **must** change. Again I told him it wasn't good enough and he left only to come back the next day with another list. Again, I told him it wasn't good enough and that I wasn't interested in helping him. I wanted to help him, but I knew he was holding back and was only partially invested at that time. I told him when he got real with this list, then and only then would I be willing to help him.

Another day passed and I saw him coming down the road toward my office. He waved to me and I waved back and he asked me to wait for him, he needed to talk. After he approached me, I went over his new list and read every word and once again I told him that he wasn't ready. He got up in my face and with more conviction than I had ever seen; he said, "You don't understand, I have to change".

I believe that at this point, we both knew that if I didn't help him he wouldn't live much longer. He explained to me that the pain was too much for him to live with, that he would do whatever he needed to do to change. How is that for wanting to make a change? Now he **needed** to change.

Part of our agreement was that he could not have a drink for 24 hours before I would work with him. He immediately explained that he knew that, and he said "I have not had a drink in over 30 hours. At that time I agreed to help him. Four hours later he quit drinking forever.

Beer was his drug of choice and I told him that beer would make him sick if he started drinking again. To his surprise, immediately after our session I handed him a can of his favorite beer and told him to drink it. I told him he would never know if what we had done worked without drinking a beer. He repeatedly refused the beer, but I insisted. He reluctantly tasted the beer and kept saying that "this beer tastes like **SHIT**", his words not mine. Within ten minutes of drinking a little beer, he began vomiting; his mind had rejected the poison of the alcohol.

Eight months later, New Year's Eve, Kenny had gone back to his hometown and that night went to his favorite bar to visit with friends and have a Pepsi. It was midnight, Happy New Year! One of his old girlfriends came over and gave him a New Year's kiss. It must've been pretty good or at least that's what he told me. She had been drinking beer, and within a few seconds after the kiss, Kenny was in the men's room vomiting. His mind told him that the taste of beer was poison. Over the next ten to fifteen years I would touch base with Kenny and he would share with me that he hadn't had the urge to drink again.

The rest of the story is that Kenny had been in five different rehabs before we met. He was labeled as an alcoholic and drug addict, and in his mind he knew he would always be one. If you were to ask him today, are you an alcoholic he would say no "I am not". For years he told people how quitting alcohol and drugs was the easiest thing he'd ever done.

This story took place in 2005.

I met a man who was addicted to almost every drug he could get his hands on. Honestly, he was also addicted to not facing his own reality. He used any drug he could get to make himself feel better. He was trying to escape the pain and seek pleasure by using drugs, but that only caused him ultimate pain.

The process began the same way as most of the other ones. I asked him, what do you want ultimately? I asked the question as if he knew what he wanted and why did he continue to use drugs? He explained that withdrawal was living hell and that every time he did it he swore he would never do drugs again, only to return to the drug scene.

He went to rehab got out and failed again, and again and again. Rehab was a painful experience, repeated too often. So the reason he didn't quit drugs was because it was too much pain to quit. So his subconscious mind kept telling him, if you quit its ultimate pain. So the reality is that the part of the brain that wants us to avoid pain was actually killing him.

I told him what he needed to do was to change his thinking process. I encouraged him to make a list of what would happen if he continued using drugs. How long would it take for the drugs to kill him? How this would devastate his wife, his family and friends. I had him to write down what it would do to his health if he continued. What were the consequences in sharing needles, which by the way he did? He called me about three hours later crying on the phone saying that he couldn't continue this way, things had to change. I told him that we could make an appointment but I wouldn't be able to see him for a few weeks as my schedule was full. He said no, I'm coming in now to see you and I don't care how long I have to wait, but I'm not leaving until you help me.

I informed him of my hourly rate and when he arrived he had $200 in small bills and the title to his car. I knew immediately that he was serious. Talk about pain, this guy had so much pain that he had to change. In fact he was willing to give me his car.

We worked together for the next two and half hours. Because his addictions were so severe I agreed to a couple of follow-up sessions. He had no idea what they would be like and I wanted it that way.

In the follow-up sessions, all I did was talk with him about the pleasure of staying clean and how his life was changing. After the second session I gave him back the title to his car and his money. He said I owe you more than that, I owe you my life. I hugged him and sent him on his way. To this day I hear from him from time to time. He's doing great, has his own business and has helped other people using the technique I've described.

THE NEXT STORY

T his story took place in August 1992. My client at the time weighed well over 284 pounds and at 5'11", that's morbidly obese, which could lead to a much shortened life. He wore slacks that had a 48 inch waist, and his suits were a size 48 as well. His doctor told him that he had high blood pressure, was pre-diabetic and is virtually guaranteed to have a massive heart attack if he didn't make some changes. His cholesterol was over 350 and his resting heart rate was over 90. His family history indicated that he would get diabetes and die in a few short years. At that time both of his brothers had been diagnosed with diabetes and heart disease before the age of 40. Sadly his older brother died from a massive heart attack due to his unhealthy life style. Sparing you all of the details, my client **NEEDED** to change if he wanted to live past 45 years old.

The process was simple, and the same one I've used for years. Write down and feel the emotional pain that his current behavior was causing him now and in his future. So for 40 minutes he began writing all the pain this would cost him.

He was a successful man with a great business, traveling around the world, eating in the finest restaurants, yet he was extremely unhealthy. If he continued with this unhealthy lifestyle he would surely die leaving behind a wife and three sons. He also did no exercise.

After the 40 minutes of intense emotional pain, seeing, visualizing how this destructive eating patterns and lifestyle would devastate his family and himself, change was simple. After feeling the pain, the same was done for pleasure. The next 20 minutes was spent writing down and then visualizing the rewards that change had made through this process. Notice I said "had made", not would make. After feeling the changes that were made, seeing his life as a healthy person, living a long life, seeing his children get married with children of their own, being a grandfather with lots of energy the transformation was complete.

This client within one year lost over 80 pounds without ever dieting. He worked out on a Nordic-track elliptical machine daily and reduced his resting heart rate below 50. His blood test came back normal and as his doctor said "this is the most amazing turnaround I've ever seen". This was done by feeling and visualizing the intense pain that the negative behavior of overeating was causing, and would have continued to cause in the future had the behavior not stopped. And then, visualizing what the future would look like now that the change was made.

The fact is this is my story! I'm healthier than I've ever been. I eat a proper diet; I exercise daily and get proper rest. Yes, I'm a walking example of how effective this process works. All because I was willing to face the pain of my past and make the conscience decision to change.

THE BEST SUCCESS STORY

The newest and best success story is about a person who read this book, did the work needed and listened to the audios. It happened so fast.

They sat down and began to "feel" for the first time in a long time, the pain that they had caused themselves and others. After writing down all the painful actions that they had created and "feeling" the pain the emotions were heartbreaking and real. Uncontrollable tears and shaking occurred all do to the realization of the pain.

So now that we've identified the pain let's transition from pain to pleasure, using the same process. The emotions that erupted from this person was from sheer pleasure, crying, laughing, and smiling from ear to ear. A few weeks, months and years later they were so appreciative of my time and this process. Finally, life has changed and they're now clean, sober and so happy to be living the life that they only imagined.

This person is **YOU**, and I want to add your success story to this book!

Zero Addiction, Zero Desire!

Welcome back to life as it should be lived.

Make the commitment to change, follow the steps and a new life will be yours, TODAY!

I want to add you to the next printing of this book, so let me know about your successes.

addictionhacks1@gmail.com

SECTION 2

The final step to recovery, the work.

SETTING CLEAR OUTCOMES

N otice that I said outcomes and not goals. The reason for the distinction is we have all failed at reaching our goals, but in every instance, we have always had an outcome. Although this seems small and insignificant, just changing that one word can dramatically improve your results.

So, what is the outcome you would like to have by reading this book, listening to the audios or getting a coach?

Generally when I've asked clients this question, they look at me bewildered, as if I didn't know what outcome they truly wanted. The fact is I really don't know what they want. Basic human nature would say we all want security, love-connection, and significance, just to mention three of the six needs. But what do you truly want?

If I asked an alcoholic what do they want, chances are they would say "I would like to stop drinking", "I don't want to feel the urge to drink anymore". But is that what they really want?

Most often the excessive drinking, drug use and over eating etc. are symptoms of a need to avoid pain most likely. So what do they truly want? The answers I've been given after my clients have really thought about this have been, I want a better relationship with my family, I want my health back so I can see my children grow and get married. I want to prove to myself and others that I can do this, and I'm not a loser. This list can be endless yet it always goes back to meeting our needs. What is your need? What are you missing in life? What could you be missing in life? At this point I recommend sitting down with a pad of paper and begin writing your feelings about your current situation. For some people this is the most difficult part of this process; facing your feelings, not your needs or wants, but your feelings.

When I work with clients, I tell them they must be clean for at least 24 hours to begin this process. Always seek the advice of a medical professional prior to beginning this process. After writing several pages of feelings it becomes evident and apparent that there's an underlying theme to their substance abuse. Sometimes its fear, anger, regret and the list goes on and on. Sometimes it's about themselves or other people, or a combination of the two but there's always a common theme.

Once you've written your feelings down, I recommend you circle or highlight the ones that have the most power. Which one has the most power and emotion for you? Although they both are in the same category, one has more emotion and power, and the other is just intellectual and factual.

You'll notice as you go along there will be a pattern in your writing and you'll know what has caused you the most pain. This is not about other people's pain that you may have caused, *this is about your pain*. If you focus on other people's pain, that will not help you change, only your feelings will.

So what is your desired outcome? Is it to stop drinking, doing drugs, eating too much or is it to change the behaviors of destruction that you've engaged in. Is it to be healthy both physically and mentally; is it to be spiritually connected? Let's think of it in a different way, is it really the drinking, doing drugs or over eating that's the problem or is it the after-effects? So what is your outcome?

In the back of this book I put some worksheets to help you with this process or you can go online and download the form to begin this process. Again, as I've said throughout this book if you need any assistance, send me an email addictionhacks1@gmail.com with your questions and I'll do my best to get back to you quickly.

One more thing, as you begin to write, continually ask yourself, what is my desired outcome? What do I really want? Asking simple yet powerful questions will help you crystallize your thinking and get the answers you NEED to make the most of this process. How powerful is this part of the process, well it's extremely powerful!

I've had several clients come to me after following this process only to share with me that they're lives have changed dramatically. They knew what they wanted, knew what was stopping them and knew they could make the powerful changes needed.

Aristotle, 322 BC

"It concerns us to know the purpose we seek in life, for then, like archers aiming at a definite mark, we shall be more likely to attain what we want."

WHY MUST I CHANGE?

I t is said, "We will do more to avoid pain than seek pleasure." Pain can also be defined as discomfort and fear. We're not talking about physical pain here were talking about mental pain. Things like embarrassment, not feeling good enough and accepting other people's labels that we don't like. This chapter is about "Why I **MUST** Change". This is not about why I would "like" to change or "maybe someday" in the future I'll change. This is about why I **MUST** change, and ***do it now!*** The process of change is the most difficult part yet it is one of the most rewarding.

If done correctly, it need not be done again. If you are willing to face intense emotional and mental discomfort for a small amount of time, you can and will change. It is said that the part of our brain known as the "reptilian brain", has one job and that is to protect us, thereby ensuring our survival. For millions of years, this part of our brain, which is on autopilot and is our subconscious, has controlled us and our reactions without us being consciously aware of it.

Our basic human survival instinct is to avoid pain and discomfort so by engaging this powerful part of our brain the part which is responsible for keeping us safe we can make massive changes in our life quickly. So, if our subconscious is there to protect us then why would we want to use it? …Because it works!

Now that you've completed the pain and discomfort process you'll be happy to know that it's time to shift into the pleasure aspect of your life. This portion of the process will help you visualize the life that you would *like* to have. Notice I said you would *like* to have, I did not say you **_need_** to have. The human brain is programmed in such a way, that we **_MUST_** avoid pain and **seek** pleasure. If this is the case, why would we continue to abuse our bodies with drugs, alcohol, excessive eating, smoking pot and or cigarettes, why do we indulge in these abusive activities that are not in our own best interest?

This next statement may seem crazy, but it's as sane as anything I've said. I bet the first time you decided to smoke cigarettes or smoke your first joint you weren't aware of the consequences. The burning chest and coughing uncontrollably; from there you went for your first alcoholic drink; oh how refreshing or at least that's what you thought at first until, not realizing that you had overindulged and suddenly the room began to spin and your insides erupted everywhere, and not long after that you found yourself lying on the bathroom floor…..so much for pleasure!

You see we use these vices to avoid <u>pain and seek</u> pleasure. The reality was you were seeking pleasure and trying to avoid pain. You may have been with friends and wanted to be cool, fit in, or wanted to mirror your parents. Quite often, to avoid pain from our past or present we try to alter our consciousness, never thinking it was going to be a lifelong addiction that leads to incredible pain. But as we began the process we've let our brain know that this abuse feels good. I have to get used to the smoke in my lungs, the alcohol in my system, the drugs that I'm using and the excessive food I'm eating, because this is actually good for me and is pleasurable. Really, nothing could be further from the truth.

So how do we use the pain to help us move forward with our changes? I highly recommend this as a two-stage process. First get out a sheet of paper and at the top of the paper, write "Why I Must Change". (See worksheet in the back of the book) Now we're assuming that you know what you want to change and the fact that you are reading this book proves you want to change something. Underneath, write down all the reasons why you must change. Don't write down why you would like to, write down why you **MUST** change. What is this costing you? What is this costing your family? What is this costing your friends? What will this cost you if you don't change? Dig deep here, think about the reality of your behavior and accept responsibility for where you are at this very moment. Allow yourself to feel the emotions after all these are your feelings......this is your life!

When I was told I was a diabetic, after rejecting immediately what the doctor said to me and his label for me, I went home and wrote down a list of the pain that being a diabetic would have cost me. I wrote down things such as I would lose my eyesight, my legs would be amputated, I would have to give myself shots every day and my life would be shortened by decades.

This pain was so real and devastating that I literally changed my eating habits at that very moment. Writing down the pain that this will cost you is useless unless it is accompanied by emotions. I could've written down anything and not attached any emotions to the process, and this would have been worthless. As I was writing I felt every word I wrote, there were tears dripping from my eyes and my entire body began to shake and shivered. I had to change or die.

The audio package has a guided meditation and workbooks to help you with this process. I use this with my coaching clients for massive change. By doing this, our brain is wired to avoid the pain. You won't have to think about avoiding the drugs, alcohol, food, and sugar etc. it will be automatic.

If you like a little help with this section please feel free to email me and I'll be happy to speak with you about your particular situation. addictionhacks1@gmail.com

This is part of the process that I've used with alcoholics and drug (OxyContin and others) addicted people to mention a few. This process works every time provided the persons **needs** have been identified and the whys they **must** change. It's been said how many psychiatrists does it take to change a lightbulb, only one, but the light bulb must want to change. In your case, "wanting to change" is not good enough. **NEED** and **MUST** are **required**. Do this exercise and you will get to a place in your life, where **need** and **must**, will propel you to success.

Sometimes I'm asked how long this process takes. The answer can vary but generally it takes 30 minutes to prepare yourself and then another 40 to 60 minutes to complete the process. In the audio version complete with the workbook, I recommend spending time writing down the reasons you must make the change, the reasons why you must quit. Then using the audio meditation, allow yourself to feel the pain make it as real as possible.

Just remember as human beings we will do more to avoid pain than to seek pleasure. The second part is the same as the first except that we will feel the pleasure of Zero Addiction.

WORKSHEET 1

What's good in my life?

Before you begin, go to a quiet safe place, free of interruptions and distractions, where you can think and begin writing undisturbed for at *"least"* one hour. If listening to music helps you, bring an iPod with you or whatever you need for listening. Ideally the music you listen to should be emotionally uplifting and not associated with any past negative memories or failures.

You should bring with you a notebook or as I like to call it a success journal. If a question can be answered multiple times, I recommend striving for 20 to 50 answers each. In my experience the best answers, the most inspiring, and the ones that have been hidden in your mind, usually come between answers number 20 and 40.

You are worth the investment of time, so no shortcuts. As always, if you have questions about this process, send me an email and I'll try to answer it as soon as possible. If during this process a negative thought or emotion pops up, thank your brain for letting you know about it, and say to your brain "I don't need that at this time in my life". This may sound simplistic but it's not. We are reprogramming your brain for ultimate success.

As Bill Bartmann says "it's time to be honest, not modest" and "get it right in your head – and you'll get it right in your life".

Remember, to answer each question at least 20 times, and always answer with a positive answer. Some of the questions may seem to be repeated, but there is a reason for this, so answer them again and again as they come up.

USE THIS FORMAT/ GUIDE

1.
2.
3.
4.
5.
6.
7.
8.
9.
10.
11.
12.
13.
14.
15.

PARENTS, TEACHERS, OTHER ADULTS

- As a child, what were the best things said about you?

- What did they say about you?

- When did it happen?

- Where did it happen?

- How did this make you feel?

- How does it make you feel now?

- What did your parent's friend or another adult about you that was positive, uplifting and nice?

- Who said it?

- Do you remember when you heard this?

- How did it make you feel?

- As a young child, what was the best thing that ever happened to you?

- As a young child, what did you accomplish? (Did you learn to walk, talk, ride a tricycle or bicycle)

- Do you remember where and when these happened? Write all of them down.

- As a child, what were the nicest complements you received? By who?

- How did these complements make you feel?

Remember, to answer each question at least 20 times, and always answer with a positive answer. Some of the questions may seem to be repeated, but there is a reason for this, so answer them again and again as they come up.

USE THIS FORMAT/ GUIDE

1.

2.

3.

4.

5.

6.

7.

8.

9.

10.

11.

12.

13.

14.

15.

BROTHER, SISTER, FRIENDS AND OTHER FAMILY MEMBERS

- As a child and young adult, what were the best things said about you by your brother, sister, friends?

- What did they say about you?

- When did it happen?

- Where did it happen?

- How did this make you feel?

- How does it make you feel now?

- What did they say about you that were positive, uplifting and nice?

- Who said it?

- Do you remember when you heard this?

- How did it make you feel?

- What was the best thing that ever happened to you as a young person?

- As a young person, what did you accomplish? (Did you learn to read, play a musical instrument, drive a car, you get the idea)

- Do you remember where and when these accomplishments happened?

- As a young person, what were the nicest complements you received?

- By who?

- How did these complements make you feel?

SUCCESSES

- As a child or young adult what successes did you have?

- Did you learn to walk?

- Did you learn to talk?

- Can you speak more than one language?

- Did you learn to write?

- Did you learn to print or write in cursive?

- Did you learn to spell?

- Did you learn to read?

- Did you learn to ride a bicycle, tricycle or scooter?

- Did you learn to swim, float on your back?

- Did you learn to dress yourself, brush your teeth?

- Did you learn to use the toilet by yourself?

    Remember not everyone can do every one of these things. Every one of these is a success that you learned to do. Do not shortchange yourself here!

- Did you learn to drive a car or motor vehicle? (If you did, you had to learn to read, write, take a test and remember the answers. Again, you weren't born with these skill)

- Do you have any "good" friends?

- What are their names?

- What complements have your good friends said about you?

- Did you have friends in the past?

- What are their names?

- What have these friends said about you that made you feel good

Remember, to answer each question at least 20 times, and always answer with a positive answer. Some of the questions may seem to be repeated, but there is a reason for this, so answer them again and again as they come up.

LOOKING FORWARD FROM TODAY WHAT WOULD YOU LIKE THESE PEOPLE TO SAY ABOUT YOU?

Remember, to answer each question at least 20 times per person, and always answer with a positive answer.

Every one of these answers can happen. Your mind could not have given you the answers, if it were not possible. Answering these questions will also lead you to an outcome of who you will become!

Congratulations!!!

WORKSHEET 2

WHY I MUST CHANGE AND WHAT IT WILL COST ME IF I DON'T

B efore beginning this section it is imperative that you are in a good state of mind. What do I mean by that, simply put, this is the most difficult, heart wrenching, and mentally painful part of the program and before beginning you must know, *__you can and will be successful.__* For some of my clients, I recommend doing this section in the presence of a therapist, a close non–judgmental friend, non-judgmental family member, or someone who can comfort you, if needed. Make no mistake about this, to be effective this section will create massive amounts of mental anguish and pain.

Depending on your addiction circumstances, now and in the past this process can take anywhere between 30 minutes to two hours. The good news here is when done correctly, this "pain" section, need only be done once. After this section, you will immediately begin the "pleasure" section of this program. Additionally, you will continue to do the "pleasure" section for years to come. Imagine that for just a moment, living in pleasure the rest of your life.

For you to begin, go to a quiet safe place, free of interruptions and distractions where you can think, feel heavy emotions and begin writing undisturbed for at *"least"* one hour. This safe place should be one were not only will you be undisturbed, but you will not disturb others. Most times when people begin to do the work they start crying, sobbing uncontrollably, shaking and otherwise feel physically horrible. If you do this around other people who are not aware of your current situation and what you are doing, it can be very disturbing.

Unlike the previous section, I highly recommend against listening to music. There are a lot of reasons for this, but just take my advice. No music.

You have with you a separate notebook to answer questions, and write down your feelings multiple times, I recommend writing down as many feelings and answers as you can. In my experience the best answers, the most painful, and the ones that have been hidden in your mind, usually come to you after just a few minutes of thinking and feeling.

You are worth the investment of time, so no shortcuts. As always, if you have questions about this process, send me an email and I'll try to answer it as soon as possible. If you are working with a therapist, psychologist or other mental health professionals please give them my contact information, and I'll be glad to answer any of their questions.

This section is about creating pain, make no mistake about that. We will do far more to avoid pain than seek pleasure. Why is this so powerful, because our brain will do almost anything to avoid pain? So if you spend an hour in extreme mental anguish, and change your life in the process, isn't it worth it?

Let's begin, I'll ask you some questions, and you can begin to write the answers. If you come up with additional answers are questions feel free to write them down. The key here is not to just write them down but, to *Feel* the answers. This is where the change happens, and happens rapidly.

THE PAST

Looking back at your addiction, what has it cost you, what has it destroyed?

- How many friendships has it destroyed? Add them up!

- Who were they? List them, one by one.

- How many other relationships has it destroyed?

- Who were they? List them, one by one.

- How many family members have been hurt by your addiction?

- Who are they? List them, one by one.

- How did this addiction destroy these relationships? List them, one by one.

*Remember to **feel** your emotions!*

- What have you taken or stolen from each and every one of them? Time, money, peace of mind, things of value? List them, one by one.

- What pain have you caused each and every one of these people? List them, one by one.

*Remember to **feel** your emotions!*

- What pain are you continuing to cause each and every one of these people? List them, one by one.

- What pains have you caused yourself in each of these relationships? List each relationship one by one, and the pains you have and still are causing yourself.

- What do these former "friends" think about you now? List them, one by one.

- Do these former "friends" want to be friends with you, while you're still addicted?

- What other people have been hurt by your addiction? List them, one by one.

- What pain have you caused the people you've hurt along the route? List them, one by one, and the pain you've caused them.

WORKSHEET 3

Afty you have completed worksheet one and two you can begin on this worksheet. If you have just completed worksheet number two I highly recommend you do some sort of physical activity for a few minutes.

What I prefer my clients to do is to stand up tall, spread your arms wide, tilt your head back while looking up and make a big crazy smile while making crazy silly noises. Do these until you laugh at how funny this seems. This may seem silly to you, but, you're signaling your brain that you're feeling good. Don't skip on this little exercise. You can also do jumping jacks, run in place for a minute or do squats, but if you do force yourself to smile. By smiling you are signaling your brain that there is and will be pleasure in your future.

If you like music, play music that is upbeat and has no negative memories from the past. You have faced the pain in worksheet number two and now it's time for a compelling, pleasurable and exciting future.

When doing this exercise it is vitally important that you do it *knowing, understanding, accepting and believing that as of today and at this very moment you have changed, forever.*

Read that last sentence once again!

Have your success journal ready and begin by writing the questions first, then the answers. When a question can be answered more than one time, I highly recommend trying to find 20+ answers. Most times the most profound and important answers are after 15 to 20 answers.

Questions

How do I feel now that I have changed **TODAY?**

Remember to "feel" the answers in your mind/body!

- Will I feel better tomorrow with the changes I've made?

- How will my body begin healing today and tomorrow and every day afterwards?

- How will my mind begun to improve?

- How will I begin to feel physically?

- How will my muscles and nerves begin to heal?

- How will my spirit improve?

- How will my attitude improve?

- How will my self-esteem improve, knowing that I'm a changed person?

- What will I do today to improve myself?

- What will I say to myself that is positive, uplifting and inspiring?

- How many times a day will I say this to myself, 100, 200, possibly 300 times?

- Now that I have changed, **how will next week look?**

- How is this week different from last week, how do I feel?

- How has my body begun to heal?

- How has my mind begun to improve?

- How do I feel physically?

- How have my muscles and nerves begun to heal?

- How has my spirit improved?

- How has my attitude improved?

- How has my self-esteem improved, knowing that I'm a change person?

- What do I do next week to improve myself further?

- What will I say to myself that inspires me to be a better person?

- How many times a day will I say this to myself, 100, 200, possibly 300 times?

- Now that I've changed, **how can I improve next month?**

Use the same set of questions as above only changing the time frame.

- Now that I have changed, what changes would I like to see in the next in **6 months?**

- Now that I have changed, **how do I feel now?**

- **Next Year** what changes would I like to see?

  Use the same set of questions as above only changing the time frame.

- Now that I have changed: Let's look at the years ahead and dream a bit: **what would it look like in 2, 3, 5 and 10 Years from now?**

- Use the same set of questions as above only changing the time frame.

At this time you might be surprised to know that the changes you imagined will for the most part, become reality. If you can imagine it, you can achieve it. Like always, if you need help with this please send me an email and I will get back to you soon as possible.

Don't make this process complicated; it's very simple, not easy but **simple.** I also recommend any time you feel you need reinforcement use this worksheet or something similar that you yourself can design. Just ask positive questions that require positive answers. Writing down the question, and answering each one of them in writing. Always try for 20 answers or more.

HOW TO MAKE CHANGE LAST

At this point I'm assuming that you've done the work outlined in this book. If I had been coaching you, you would've had tremendous breakthroughs at this stage of your life. You would have felt the pain of the past and the pain of what could've been your future. This would not have just been an intellectual experience but, a very emotional one as well. You also would have experienced intense pleasure knowing how your life has progressed and where you're headed.

How do we make this change last?

Do we want to revisit the past, no way! Remember, you're now driving your life car looking through the front windshield, not in the rearview mirror. So we will, in our minds and hearts seek, a compelling future, one that meets all of our needs, wants and desires.

The best way to continue your positive journey is by reinforcing the good experience. Just as you have lived in the past, as we all have, why not experience the future now, why wait? If you spend time daily reinforcing the great feelings and seeing the future in advance, your progress will be fast and permanent. If you think this is crazy than think again. You will be in great company. People like Thomas Edison, Henry Ford, Einstein, Bill Gates, Elon Musk and countless others have done this and many still are. The book "Think and Grow Rich" is about this very exercise. *Now, Do IT!*

How to Do This for a Lasting Positive Impact

I'm not sure of your primary mode of communication is visual, auditory or kinesthetic so at this point you'll have to be the driver of your own life. If you go to the end of this book, there is a quiz called "VAK". Take the test to identify what your primary mode of communication skills are.

If you are auditory, that is you like to listen to things, then you should make your own personal recording that includes (in your own voice) positive affirmations, visualizations from your future and some uplifting music in the background. Saying things like "I am living a life that's fulfilled, happy and successful". Now at this point I must emphasize, you do not want to add things such as I "no longer" drink alcohol or I am drug-free. Your mind will grab onto the words, drink alcohol and drugs and will not help you with your change. No mention of where you've been should be in your affirmations, only where you're going. If you need help with this, send me an email of what you've written and I will be happy to help you write the story of your life in advance. addictionhacks1@gmail.com. In the subject line, write "Affirmations".

If you are visual, that is you like to look at things, you can make a slideshow as a screen saver. Or make a DVD for your TV with incredible images and some visions of the life that that you've chosen to live. On each one of the slides you could add words like I'm confident, I'm inspired, I'm happy, I'm successful, I'm a great husband/wife. *Never* add words from your past such as I am "no longer" an alcoholic or drug user. Again, your brain will only see the negative side of your past not the positive side of your future. I have included the "rules" of positive affirmations at the end of this chapter to assist you in the process.

And finally, <u>if you are kinesthetic</u> (frankly, I think everyone should do this regardless of learning styles) I would advise purchasing a journal or note book and every morning and afternoon write the answers to some "compelling" questions such as, who loves me, who do I love? What's great in my life right now, and what will or could be great in my life right now? What's funny about this situation? The best part of this is you get to decide the questions, so ask positive questions that can only be answered with a positive answer.

Why is …. so great for me?

Why do I ALWAYS do great at…..?

What is great in my life NOW?

What "could" be great in my life?

Hum, think about that question for a moment. Life at this second may not be great but, asking the right question will help you see the positive outcomes you will have in the future. Do you have eyes, feet, arms that work?

If making the audio or the "movie" DVD is difficult for any reason, let me know as I work with a team of visual artist and audio engineers who can do this for you and skyrocket your results.

RULES OF AFFIRMATIONS

- Affirmations must be in the positive.
- Never refer to any past addiction i.e. never say:
  - o I'm no longer addict or I'm no longer a....
    (whatever label you accepted for yourself).
  - o I'm no longer overweight or an alcoholic....
- Always refer to the present and the future.
  - o I am living a healthy life. As an example you
    could say, every day, and every way, my life is
    getting better.
  - o At this point say out loud specific things that
    are improving, even if they are small! Do this
    with emotions.
- Decide what you want to change and make a statement
  that supports positive change in your life. For example
  you could say:
  - o Finally I'm living an incredibly healthy life,
    enjoying healthy foods and getting healthier

day by day. Do Not Say, living healthy and <u>not doing drugs,</u> alcohol etc.

- Again, you can send an email and I will look it over for you.

HUMAN NEEDS

This is from the Tony Robbins website you should print it, keep it with you and review it several times a day for the next few weeks. You will then understand at your deepest level, why you do the things you do.

For the record, I'm not associated with nor have any financial interest in any of Tony Robbins companies or products. I know from experience that his work has helped millions of people have a better life, including mine and some of my family member.

THE SIX HUMAN NEEDS

1. **Certainty**: assurance you can avoid pain and gain pleasure

2. **Uncertainty/Variety**: the need for the unknown, change, new stimuli

3. **Significance**: feeling unique, important, special or needed

4. **Connection/Love:** a strong feeling of closeness or union with someone or something

5. **Growth**: an expansion of capacity, capability or understanding

6. **Contribution:** a sense of service and focus on helping, giving to and supporting others

I highly recommend Tony Robbins seminars. He has a three day weekend program that has significantly changed the lives of many. These programs have been life-changing for many people.

https://www.tonyrobbins.com/

BONUS SECTION, YOUR LEARNING STYLE

This section contains a test called the VAK test. It stands for visual, auditory and kinesthetic. We all have different primary and secondary methods of learning. Some of us are extreme visual learners, others learn by listening and hearing and others primarily by touching and feeling.

Each one of these "learning styles" is unique to each of us individually. But in one way or another we use each one of the styles to learn. Which one is your primary, your secondary and finally your third learning style?

Knowing this, and then using this knowledge, will dramatically improve your life and learning abilities. In this book, (ADDICTION-HACKS ©) I recommend creating your own voice recording, visual memory board or display what you want your future to be like. Crafting your vision, using your primary and secondary learning styles will exponentially enhance your results.

In 2018 I hired a PhD in clinical psychology to create a test to find a person's learning style. This test was administered to several hundred people to verify the accuracy. When I saw the test results I was shocked, over 98% of those who took the test proved how accurate the test was. As a comparison, the first standardize test which consisted of 200 questions was no more accurate. This simple test will be your guide to how you learn. Consider this test my gift! As always should you have any questions, email me, I'll be happy to try to help you.

Visual, Auditory, and Kinesthetic (VAK) Learning Styles Test

William Nixon © 2019

Please circle or highlight the letter/sentence with the response that mostly applies to you.

1. When reviewing for an exam you tend to:

   - record the information and listen to it

   - highlight, underline, and reread

   - rewrite concepts or pace around

2. You usually spend your free time:

   - dancing, playing sports, working out

   - singing, talking with friends,

   - painting, drawing, watching, taking photographs, writing

3. When finding your way to a certain address you tend to:

   - use a map/ GPS or phone

   - ask directions from someone

   - use your instinct by trying different routes

4. When assembling furniture or equipment you:

   - refer to the diagrams in the manual

   - use trial and error or approximate where each piece fits

   - call someone to explain the process

5. When a song is being played, you often:

   - pay attention to the pitch, tone, and melody

   - imagine what the singer looks like

   - move or dance to the rhythm

6. During boring lectures, you tend to:

   - listen to music or sing to myself

   - doodle, draw, or daydream

   - fidget or fiddle with something

7. In cooking or preparing new dishes, you first:

   - watch or read the procedure

   - talk through the steps in your head or with someone

- taste the dish or finished product and experiment with the ingredients

8. Five minutes before an important interview, you would probably:

  - practice your smile or check how you look

  - clear your throat and take note of the quality of your voice

  - take deep breaths and maintain a smart posture

9. You can better focus on something when it is:

  - loud enough or musical

  - colorful or aesthetic

  - moving or active

10. Your attention is usually taken by people who:

  - talk or express themselves

  - look pleasant or attractive

  - move with confidence

11. When weighing decisions, you:

  - list pros and cons

  - use your gut-feel

  - listen to what others think about it

12. When teaching a skill, you prefer to:

    - demonstrate the process or techniques

    - talk about the strategies and entertain questions

    - use pictures, videos, diagrams, and other illustrations

13. You think a person is lying if:

    - he talks in a higher pitch or shaky voice

    - he cannot keep still and maintain eye contact

    - my gut says so

14. Looking back at grade school, you can vividly remember:

    - your classmates' faces; the colorful rooms/ halls

    - your classmate's voices; the ringing or buzzing bells or tones

    - the games you played, your favorite lunch or snack

VAK-SCORING:

Indicate whether your answer in each item is V (visual), A (auditory), or K (kinesthetic) V.A.K Learning Styles Test

1. When reviewing for an exam you tend to:

   - Record the information and listen to it   :A

   - Highlight, underline, and reread   :V

   - Rewrite concepts or pace around   :K

2. You usually spend your free time:

   - Dancing, playing sports, working out   :K

   - Singing, talking with friends   :A

   - Painting, drawing, watching, writing   :V

3. When finding your way to a certain address, you tend to:

- Use a GPS or map   :V

- Ask someone for directions   :A

- Use your instinct by trying different routes   :K

-

4. In assembling furniture or equipment, you:

- Refer to the diagrams in the manual   :A

- Use trial and error or approximate where

   each piece fits   :V

- Call an expert to explain the process   :K

5. When a song is being played, you often:

- Pay attention to the pitch, tone, and melody   :A

- Imagine how the singer looks   :V

- Move or dance to the rhythm   :K

6. During boring lectures, you tend to:

- Listen to music or sing to myself   :A

- Doodle, draw, or daydream   :V

- Fidget or fiddle with something   :K

7. In cooking or preparing new dishes, you first:

- Watch or read the procedure   :V

- Talk through the steps in your head or with someone :A

- Taste the dish or finished product and experiment with the ingredients :K

8. Five minutes before an important interview, you would probably:

   - Practice a smile or check how you look :V

   - Clear your throat and take notes of the quality of your voice :A

   - Take deep breathes and maintain a smart posture :K

9. You can better focus on something when it is:

   - Loud enough or musical :A

   - Colorful or aesthetic :V

   - Moving or active :K

10. Your favorable attention is usually taken by people who:
    - Talk or express themselves eloquently :A

    - Look pleasant or attractive :V

    - Move with confidence :K

11. When weighing decisions, you:
    - List pros and cons :V

    - Use your gut-feeling :K

    - Listen to what others think about it :A

12. When teaching a skill, you prefer to:

   - Demonstrate the process or techniques :K

   - Talk about the strategies and entertain questions :A

   - Use pictures, videos, diagrams, and other illustrations :V

13. Looking back at grade school, you can vividly remember:

   - Your classmates faces; the colorful rooms :V

   - Your classmates voices; the ringing or buzzing of the bell :A

   - The games you played, your favorite lunch or snack :K

Count the frequency of your responses and fill out the table below:

Learning Style	Visual (V)	Kinesthetic (K)	Auditory (A)
SUM			

The column with the highest sum reflects your primary learning style. The second highest total is your secondary learning style and the third your least dominate learning style.

www.ingramcontent.com/pod-product-compliance
Lightning Source LLC
Chambersburg PA
CBHW060951040426
42445CB00011B/1103